     Ink by Verena Raban on pages 11, 16, 36
     Collage by Katie Erbs on page 58
     Pen and Pencil by Kim Wylie on page 52

Graphic Design by Tyler Mohesky and Kate Wylie

Printed in The United States of America

TABLE OF CONTENTS

FLOWERMOUTH

New and Selected Poems

KATE WYLIE

NO MORE MARTYRS

OUTSIDE THE REDWING SHOE STORE

He says I've got a lot of crazy shit
in my head. He isn't wrong. He says to put it
all down on paper, which I do. Blind woman

with a machine gun, shooting at the moon.
I buy my father a new pair of shoelaces.
He says thank you. Wants to know

how it's going. I say it's going. He nods
because he understands. It's autumn. Now
it's April, now it's yesterday. Now he's dead

and all I have are his bootprints in the sand.
Now it's raining in the desert, which I can hear
without putting my ear to the ground.

RUST BELT HIPPARCHUS

When the wind howls, he answers slow and loud.
Brother of wishbone, son of boulder and snake.
He'll bring stargazer lilies to any wake.
This is the story of Rust Belt Hipparchus:
doors opened then shut. He was lucky
to escape, counting prayer beads and stars
and windowless black cars. He hardened
then melted. He began loving wildflowers.
He dismissed a divisive mistress and now
he misses her. He dismantled his melancholy
only to take a part-time job as Head Sorrow Interpreter.
He stares at triangles all day, begging them to reconcile
with the reality of things. Wears untied sneakers
and buys his groceries from the gas station.
He haunts himself. Bites his tongue until it bleeds.
Attends weekly sessions for anger management.
Attends weekly sessions for swallowing glass swords.
Please stop hurting yourself, they beg. *We're worried.*
He doesn't listen. The whippoorwill beyond
his stained-glass window is singing again.
When it makes music, he whistles back.

Waiting for the Night
Shift Bus to Little Rock

Rusted Datsuns linger under a paint-fading sun
and the broadsides of barns are adorned
with giant acrylic American flags. Swingset
chains sigh back and forth. Children shuffle
home from school, backpacks shifting shoulder
to restless shoulder. Plastic helmets clash
as the football team takes their first of the season.
Gatorade drips red down thirsty chins.
One assistant holds a stopwatch, snapping his fingers
until everyone jogs back across the field, kicking up
little clumps of dirt. The whole town's been talking
about our prospects this year. Even the freshmen
are corn-fed and fast as hounds. When the senior
running-back got drafted, a whisper went around
our season might be shot. The quarterback
stayed home for two days and we all thought
he'd quit the team for sure. But he came back
the next day, throwing spiral after perfect
spiral. And boys keep coming
over from the middle school, every year
arriving with surer hands and fleeter feet
until even the holiest of Hail Marys feel just
like more passes, and although we lose a couple
kids every year to a war that's never won, the seasons
keep demanding champions, the buses keep arriving on time.
When the head coach blows his whistle
signaling the end of practice, players
exchange sweaty congratulations for making it
another day, then go their separate ways
through the chain-link fence surrounding the field.
Our quarterback walks the two blocks home, helmet
hanging at his side, then disappears
into a house where POW-MIA flies at half-mast
over an empty two-person cement bench
illuminated by approaching headlights.

SHADOWSONG

Standing in the middle
of our backwoods gravel road,
glacial sky refusing
any sentiment of snow, no signs
of rain, no clouds or disappearing
moon, just pitch pines stretching
on and on for miles and a doe
laboring on the shoulder, tall grass
growing all around her. I'd seen
her grazing in the willow tree grove,
stomach swelling in twilight, dark
eyes flashing at the sound of footfall.
Steam was rising from the truck's
red hood. Four thin legs extruded
from her. She pushed
once more, and finally
the fawn slid from her. Where
there should have been a flutter
of heartbeat, only stillness.
Where I prayed for a tremble
of mercy, we found none.
My only wish was to not be afraid.

Admiral Fitzroy's Storm Glass Predicts Snow in April

I can't put out birdfeed
without the whole neighborhood singing
about it. *Here comes the woman*
in her father's old tee shirts.
He isn't even dead
yet. She already mourns him.
What long shadows he will leave
at the foot of each mountain.
Time's unhinged revolving door. Acorns
grown up and down simultaneously.
The crimson wounds of wallflowers.
What spellbooks and secrets we keep.
Poor daddies. Poor grannies. See girl run.
See girl flee police.
See girl slit her wrist over the sink.
Closet the questions. My answers
will kill you. Send larkspur bending backward.
I can't shine this silverware anymore
without dogwoods glimmering
beyond the windowpane. In this instant,
future becomes past. Holy Moses,
don't let me be a ghost so soon.
Don't take the black hills and badlands
from me now. Don't take my father.
Bet my life on how fast a bad mind goes.
Give me back starlings, their merciless laughter.
Give me back those memories, tattered
clothes we never throw away. Give me lone notes
in darkness, that wayward, weathered song.

EATING GRAPE TOMATOES IN THE DARK

Standing naked in my kitchen,
half-full container in one hand
and takeout packet of salt in the other,
I'm eating my first meal in three days.

If I say I'm not hungry, is that enough?
If I tell you I don't want it?
I can't stop dreaming
about his too-real face in the casket.

If I say the body looked fake?
If I tell you the grave was shallow?
How long will you be a visitor within your own life?
Blinking neon signs demand a satisfactory answer.

The world outside is kneeling.
A glass of wine on the counter has turned.
Mud floods the blood-red fields
while my hometown chokes on codeine and cigarillo smoke.

I'm a vesper of sadness. Father, bury my faith
behind the abandoned Walgreens,
where gospels gather
every Sunday, bright posters likening

God to one of those soccer moms
toting a little monogrammed lawn chair
to match his floppy sunhat, yelling
when the referees blow a call.

MAGICIAN, MADWOMAN

I wrote the same poem thirty times.
Easter baskets, closing caskets, yellow umbrellas

turned inside-out by darkening weather.
Rain in Pittsburgh. Happy Thanksgiving.

One poem calls this sensation *magic*, the other calls it *science*.
You want them to face one another, have the discussion.

You want my poems to speak
but I was born without a mouth.

This is genetic. It's a fault.
Tomorrow I'll repent. Tomorrow I'll be better.

The grandfather clock reads 10:07 again.
Someone hangs from the penthouse window, shouting:

he loves you, sister. This I promise.
Please, God, no more martyrs.

Please keep that man from falling.
Magician, madwoman, love potion, flowermouth.

The people around us count out the year in trimesters
while we've been penny-pinching and planning funerals.

One sniff of whiskey, one touch of death.
Mouthful of ash. Fistful of coffee grounds.

Watch as I disappear behind the curtain only to return
with an armful of snowshoe hares,

how I fold myself in quarters, then quarters again
to climb inside your overstocked heart.

Watch how helpful I can be. How delicate. How ladylike.
Watch as I shrink down and down and down for you.

Take on your reflection as my own.
Two loose sequins in a torn pocket.

I make you the moonlight. Turn you into my twin.
Tomorrow, I'll beg you to split me down to the rind,

overripe orange, big brave girl, feather-light steel, and thyme.
Tomorrow we'll watch flies drop into a cup

and talk about how brave the dead can be.
I wrote the same poem thirty-one times.

The seer to her blind man. Strawberries and sunshine.
Seventy-seven degrees in November. Love should be

the least of my worries. I shouldn't worry
about love. I shouldn't even remember the word, given the world.

Ghosts rising from gold-spun evenings, bundles of roses,
two million minds gone rotten and this

synesthetic explanation: another blueberry. Another raspberry. Chalk fading
from the sidewalk. I won't even say the word. I can't pronounce it anymore.

Tomorrow I'll go back to the church of my childhood
and listen while those enormous echoes chime.

ONE-HUNDRED AND NINETEEN RIDGES ROUND THE EDGE OF EVERY AMERICAN QUARTER, WHILE PENNIES HAVE NONE

My mother the moth,
father the mountain—
counting out frustrations
with fingerpaints,
wet coloring books
cast about the yard.
Two magicians making
two more magicians,
walking the world
blue-eyed and broken.
My mother the ocean,
father the sailor—
buying magazines
for one another
even after the divorce.
She gets People.
He, National Geographic's
Special on the Dead
Sea Scrolls. Unravels
constellations in his mind.
How do you rationalize
parents loving one another
enough to buy groceries
but not cook breakfast?
My mother the fractured,
father the fixer—
he who could mend
anything, except for her.
How do you rationalize
a lover's pride? How
do you kneel and beg
forgiveness? Slice a fig
without using your tongue?
After forty years

of uneven twilight
and unasked questions, how
do you repair something
refusing to be seen?
Take it in your hands.
My father the lasso,
mother the meadow—
her tears were horses
and she released them.

Super 8

Peace treaties rewrite themselves
here, in the middle ground, across
from Waffle House and Home Depot,
where the billiard ball sign floats
bloated as unsatisfied Chaplain Moon.
Howl-choked wolves skulk dark dumpsters
emitting stale scents of butter and ham,
crusts and cigarette butts. This is where
shattered beer bottles come back together.
Adam stands alone on the balcony, smoking a Santa Fe.
He tries to identify each bird in the branches,
call them by monikers he can understand:
Hushed; Atomic; Sound of Tomorrow.
Behind him, Eve appears
from an unlit doorway, thin body
slightly bent and metallic as a hanger, holding up
the tattered silk underdress, the tattooed sparrow
on her shoulder blade already disappearing.
She knows how to pronounce
animal names in every language—even their own—
but doesn't admonish Adam for his rituals;
his sons have renamed everything
for the sake of comprehension.
Eve shakes her head when he offers a drag,
pulling a pack of American Spirits from thin mountain air.
Some understandings have no need for explanation.
In the trees, a waxwing quits eavesdropping, bids both lovers
a dulcet goodnight. Everything resolves here,
one way or another. They'll be gone
when the morning heat wave breaks
to silence every creature in the forest.
When the winged singer skeletonizes,
they'll still remember how it sounded.

WANT

I wake up with your hands in my hair
but you're not there. It's that impossible
can't stay, can't leave, can't live, can't breathe,
can't escape the pull of you, the undertow of want,
spread-eagle scent of desire, raspberry
and cinderblock—two kinds of tomorrow.
Shock of sunburn on your palms,
red wine spilled across new carpet,
fingers caught in revolving door hinges.
Diamond-encrusted pain of promise.
How joy spreads like wildfire.
Night sounds of animals along the interstate.
Days like shadows stretching across hardwood floors.
Poppyseeds between your teeth. Baptisms by fire
and this ring of thorns. Your tongue
inside my cheek. Bees and briars. Gravel
under new tires. The red rust of use.
Spoons. Sharp knives. The dull ones too.
Death made us see our lives for what they were—
evaluate the orange tree, shrubs, daylight,
any hitch-thumbed thing hiding in the weeds.
The ocean's yawn. Wide-mouthed birds diving.
A painted thoroughbred's pulse after sprints.
Fingerprints on fogged glass, pink
picnic basket overflowing with figs.
Stars and valleys—where they go every morning.
A tartan blanket wrapped around your shoulders.
Wraiths lifting from the river. Or maybe rain.
The memory of moss hanging from trees, humid
stick of loss, knuckles knocking on a chin. Bodies laid out
fresh across the field. Our hands barely touching, you said
this is either heaven or hell and we couldn't decide which.

I've Been Spending an Enraging Amount of Time with My Dreams

I can only offer an omen of cold Sunday mornings. The varicose veins
of West Texas rivers near-dry. A woman in white sifting the riverbank
for arrowheads, glint in her eyes reflecting wild water. Twice in my life,
I've watched the black boat sail away without a captain, never
    coming back
completely empty: shovel, hummingbird feeder,
    handful of watermelon seeds,
skateboard turned onto its face. But that woman in the sand belongs
to the lamplight of Autumn. She belongs to the pillar of dust just beyond
the back porch. This home becomes a conch shell. The air's sweet
    suffocating dirt.
Ashes go on glowing in the dark. Drought in the south doesn't stop
    the floodplains
from anticipating rain. Rain, rain, rain. I can only offer this
    unyielding weather.

SOL

he says i put too much "u" in it
sol sol sol he repeats and repeats
until we're lying on a bed of nails

he says *la fe muere en la oscuridad*
while mine languishes in an open window
i'm learning to pray in another language

he says he's never loved a blonde woman before
i believe him because it's easy
wild onions sprout against the house

he says corn grows taller in mexico
missouri and kansas are sisters in a hotel bed
i learn how to make mole from scratch

he says *palabras* have rigidity and *ironía* dies
telephone wires gleam with red foil balloons
the nearest coast is almost two thousand miles away

he says we need to celebrate more
mira mira mira this is my armor
tides keep sweeping seaweed away from the shore

he says being a father is hard work
and laughs when i refer to poetry as a *field*
every corner gets imperceptibly bluer

he says fate can't possibly be explained
a new moon is rising fast over the horizon
my bilingual dictionary provides no direct translation for the term *heartache*

he says we'll regret this but i do already
the past and future are colliding right now
and right now and right now and right now

he says sometimes i appear in his dreams as a white horse
i live in a wildfire meadow
where no rain falls

he says i put too much "u" in it
and after all this time
i still do

EASTER SUNDAY

Not a long-lasting candle
saved in case of natural disasters,
but one melting, brightly-colored,

down from the curved shape of a cloud.
I'll follow my father
toward a glorious death involving fire,

sky crumbling open to reveal
winged stallions cascading
through peeled, pinwheeling skeletons

pulled into midair by a twister
wider than heaven and twice as bright.
The roadside zoo outside of town

where a female bear died of loneliness
while waiting for a mate
will get swept away by sheer weather.

Nature reclaiming the landscape beneath us.
Name the storm after a woman,
blame her, then be done with it.

Let clean-up begin. Find your pet,
rebuild where you can. Somewhere
Joplin's brewing. A structure burns

with the electricity of sleeping bodies.
Harmonizing with distant thunder,
wild dogs howl for the mercy of love

while freight trains continue to roll.

Ours Poetica

In the shadow of bent steeples, downtown's grayed noon becomes night.
Blacklight and neon beckon. We stand close together while the clocktower
bemoans the hour. The sky becomes a cloak of stars. I'm homesick again.
I didn't eat dinner. We don't hold hands. I was reborn at twenty-four, then
again at twenty-five, and now this city's wrapped her hands
            around my throat, begging for change
I can't give. Bouquets of navy. Dead weight of petals
dripping off uneven blooms. Unrequited
night-songs of ambulance sirens and mourning doves. A city spring
so cold, it rusts young bones. Ovenbird and doe. High green hills
that call the cattle home. Liquid diet. Fluid foods. Or bouquets of maroon:
how to say *I cherish you*, and mean it. You taught me how to mean it.
How to be unafraid, even at the apex. Call me sentimental. Call this
confessions from the top of the Ferris wheel. Call me Icarus Barbie.
Every city is ours. Every hometown, drowned in cardinals.
Every state line shines with love and unmoved blood. Lady Liberty
wiping her eyes with the Arch's soft edges. Dangerous laughter.
The first day of April, July, September, all the same magnetic blue.
Children sent screaming through the streets, little bodies rippling
with the new season. Oversized cartoon hammers dangle from silver hooks.
Sheriffs and sailors hover over hot railings. Lemons press through
machines. Men press into me. I've been busy falling in love
with the oaks, green on fire. My friends make fun of each other
            for being too tall. Too beautiful.
We could be teens or retirees. Maybe ageless angels. Maybe twenty-two.
I'm desperate to care about anything else as much as I care about you.
The country keeps taking. I'll give and give until there's nothing left
except a carelessly stained red-and-white checked tablecloth,
four crows scrapping for hotdog buns in the overgrown grass.
We nod when people ask if we're voting. We nod when they mention kids.
We understand it's cheaper to take a limousine to the hospital
than an ambulance. We understand people leave binoculars
in the minivan. We understand why people trade hoopties for coffins.
You watched me learn to walk again; held my hand when I fell. No—
it's not hard to imagine the gun. It's not hard to imagine the grave.
We understand some people fall for good—that love can't always save.
Somewhere three-thousand miles away, my brother lifts himself
from a few paltry hours of near-dreams, returning, already, to the plastic

manufacturing plant, its fumes embedded permanently into the soft
cotton fibers of his company-issued polo, the lingering ring
around his bloodshot eyes gazing at the goggles hanging by a hook
near the front door of our father's home, where my brother still lives,
foot-sore hours amounting only to exhaustion and the question
he hears every day while leaving: *are you coming back tomorrow?*
Three-note tones chime over the factory intercom, and men pour
into snow-thick streets, shadows flickering across sober faces as they
light cigarettes for one another and cling to day-old newspapers, brown
paper bags crumpling within tight fists. The streetlights have been on
for hours. My brother comes home, unlaces the Oakleys,
falling into the twenty-year-old twin, reaching for something
none of us can see. And in the morning, he pours black coffee
into a black thermos, traverses white streets, and arrives always
fifteen minutes early, steam lifting around his muted, indifferent eyes
which know what work is. When they tell me to be sweeter, softer,
roll their eyes at my penniless pride, my wicker basket full of blue
berries picked at the base of an ancient mountain, where one side
of each bush thickens faster than the other—I think of the men
whose hands lifted me from a dozen daisy gardens, men whose days
are spent in faceless buildings, whose nights are riddled with the fire
        of dreams, and who die
before they're given the chance to indulge in nostalgia. I think of how
so few see the age where memories become currency passed carefully
from palm to smoke-cracked palm, finger joints aching from the weight
of something unspeakable. I think about Mississippi, Sister Fatima, charms,
chores, horseshoes hung over the front door. The alphabet's harassment
of linguists. Twenty-six letters strung out along a white page, wind-blown
filters drifting in a hard breeze. How the stranger brushing his teeth
in Central Park this morning looked like my neighbor back home.
I think of your sweat-spangled arms, the gleam of gravel and shovels leaning
haphazardly against the house. Sitting in the bed of my truck,
the darkness and chill of October. How I turn away when you cry.
I think about whether our future includes children. How, when women
give birth, a mother is also born. Sad historians that can't hold back blood.
I didn't understand all this before. Now I see more graves than babies.
If I say everybody's dead, you'll call me hyperbolic. But it's true:

Everybody from Bourbonville is dead now, except my brother and me.
        How so few live.
Change eats away at the soul. Termites in the skull. And I—daughter
of two crazed carpenters—want to blueprint a perfect lavender world
but can't rub two coins together. I don't want to lose you
to a crowd of ravens. Call me foolish, but every feather makes me jealous
these days. Every saltwater burn leaves a rose-colored scar.
Popsicle on my tongue too late in the season. How things end
without our knowing. The last time we walked home
from the community pool. I looked back through the gate—
desolate tetherball court, leaves and trash tangled in the bent fence.
Hand on the turnstile, wet two-piece, exposed midriff, memories
coming down hard as rain. How I kept walking anyway. Bouquets
of yellow: how fast girls grew into women those days,
when the world flung itself backward and stars misaligned.
I want to go back there, just to braid my younger self's hair.
Nothing else. I wouldn't trade my heartache for something ruby-rare.
Tonight there's a lady in the street sawing on her beat-up fiddle,
aware and unafraid of her shadow. No mockingbirds are being beaten
by fast rocks from slingshots, not by moonlight or frost
or the clouds cast down from heaven. Not the ruined church
tilted by waterfall ivy, or the cracked bell echoing melancholy tolls.

CARNIVOROUS

American Lady

In Champaign, the churches gray
and roads become long rivers

running fast with ghosts. The time-dusted
hardwood floors lament. Cold beer

bottle shards were swept into careful piles
then left behind. Each corner's shadowed over by cobwebs

while jewelry-box gems shine byzantium
and wine. Where graveyards used to be,

there's only daffodils. The whippoorwills
have disappeared. We knew they would.

American ladies stand in for them, reclaiming
empty doorframes with their bright wings,

beating the air into a hazel-fire fury,
antennas whispering an ancient worry,

one minute here, then gone.
They find another town to bury.

St. Louis Blooms

From the ground up, first
so many bodies buried by fresh
spring dirt, then lilac bushes, redbud
blossoms, bluebirds building homes
high up in purple branches. And the sky
bruising the morning, warms
from the east, brooding
and silent. The city rises
to meet darkening weather.
I'm not telling you anything
you don't already know. We sit
on the front stoop, taking in the tan
wind-tattered flower beds, dreaming
of what we'll do when spring comes singing.
*Shining blue star only shines
so long*, you whisper, leaving
an empty beer bottle on the porch.
We're trying to grow something here,
where weeds strangle everything,
America's most dangerous city five years
in a row, where perennials outlive most people
and ivy grows thicker when it's poison.

WHERE THERE'S SMOKE

When ticks bite
the sleek western fence lizard,
each becomes cured
of its otherwise lifelong sickness—
the way we were surely doomed
to decades without love
until the door shouldered open,
a summer wind blew
you into me, and suddenly
every breathing creature
this side of Seattle lifted its head.

Mirrors Where Bass Should Be

My grandmother was afraid
of the river. She doesn't approach it, even
in dreams, but comes back
to melancholy me again, shining

with shards of a wayward past—
berries, bruises, dark blue hues,
the long goodbye of blackbirds.

Cooling coffee and half-peeled nail polish,
cacophony of pool balls clacking together.
Grits in the morning, Chex Mix at night.
My grandfather wrote the Snake-Eaters Almanac,

blessed me with honeysuckle braids
shaking no at any sign of snow. Strange,
how three-dimensional daylight makes me
look. Even I can see

the splintered cello heart, hear its song
rattling around inside girlish ribs.
I wish this didn't feel so much like loss,
like becoming a woman all over again—

antique call bells ringing and ringing,
the dead doe that doesn't stay dead,
shattered coffee cup, color red.
This day blooming beyond the window,

blue-shock and brilliant.
This love song I can't seem to shake.
This memory.
This fish, dead at my fingertips.
This pair of ghosts waiting in the corner.

View-Master Vignettes

for Nigel Harris-Scott, 1995–2020

I.

Cain and Abel in cocoons,
twin blue moons, carnivorous blooms.

II.

Record-breakingly cold outside,
the riverboat casino can't even begin
it's racketed running, the wind's
swept every tree branch breathless. I wipe my nose
against my sleeve. The sun's already setting.

We've shut our lives away so long and now
they stand at the door, knocking with their fast
hard hands, flat palms demanding our attention.

So you stand up
and reach for me,
but I get up on my own
because that's the only way
I know how.

III.

Tobacco breath and breaking glass.
Wrapped around a colt 45 tall-boy and glock,
knuckles spell out *birth* and *death*.
We're living in between, not quite eighteen.
You've got a stolen bottle of blueberry vodka
tucked under your shirt. I still pray for you
every night.

IV.

Dogs in the alley fight with their teeth. It's hard pulling myself away
from cable news. Down the road, bottle rockets
burst against darkness. On the television, a cop car
upside down and burning from the inside.
Before you close the door, you turn back
and say everything's okay.
I choose to believe you.

V.

We're ten again,

      sprawled out on my dark blue rug,
      watching the stars on my ceiling glow
      sharp and cold
      then fade.

We're making friends
with darkness.

VI.

You want to be the moon,

want your bones to rise
from the dirt and dance.

You want to come
'round the mountain
riding six white horses.

> *Lord, let me watch*
> *from the height of Your shoulders.*
> *Say one word and I'll eat the earth.*

VII.

So much later, you return
as a pink-spotted hawkmoth
lighting on my hammock in the backyard.

AT THE CARNIVAL

The fortune teller extends her generous hand:
three of wands, high priestess, my prideful heart.
I fall apart before her. She strokes my hair
with glistening fingernails while the sun sets
behind the blue-and-red-shocked Ferris wheel.
Born on a leap-year sabbath to two nonbelievers,
wind-lashed and wild as tides,
I was the prodigal daughter
carrying a city in my jaws, though
we sleep where we fall in this honey-mire
heartland. There are no perfect American girls,
no sweatless cups of fat-free sun
kissed strawberry ice cream. Instead
we are razorblades on denim in your grannie's garage.
Él Volcán, the Mississippi's muddy edge, stopped clocks,
wiffle balls in the creek. We lick-shine
gold teeth, shave our heads, draw bright rings
around our eyes, and disappear
where the walls meet at a dusk-thick corner. Silences come
away from the tongue, pink bathroom sink swallowing
each earned truth. Moments become memories
in the dustbowl-dirty rearview. This is how
disaster falls on my head, fine like confetti—
gray emu egg of shame, faces turned away.
I'm stepping out of this tilted treehouse.
I never pledged allegiance or buried my dead
in graceless weeds. I'm not a rose
arguing over handguns. Floodlights
flicker. God hands out judgment
and the stars don't hide—they shine
brighter. This isn't about my mother
or the way we hurt each other, but
black cabs taking loved ones home. Delmar Boulevard
blinks back tears with broken traffic lights. As children, we learn
numbers by association with ammunition sizes, then
refuse to grow old, so our own grandparents resent us.

My father built a coffin for my eighteenth birthday.
We all agree it's best to be prepared
when the bomb drops. It has a name.
We chant it outside Lyda's place.
We know tombstones crumble and all falls
end in snow, but when the riverside shack slides
two inches downhill in a hard rain, we can't decide if it means
six more weeks of winter or the start of ruby bonnet spring.

ISAAC GODDAMN NEWTON

Apples for teeth. How
golden, this loneliness.
Wood-grained and hollow.
He's gonna heal funny.
Divorce left him limping
crooked, crowded city
sidewalks full of lovers, happy
people coupled up to ring in
another new year, fresh white
slate, harmonizing, lovely stars,
cursing the deft sound light makes
when dawn comes just to fracture
across the face he prayed for
at that exact moment night
turns to morning, doves
rise from nothing, snow banks sink back
to hell through metric tonnes of ice.
But that unbridled before
only exists in history now. Just the past.
Still, he rips the skin away. Her celestial departure—
the bed where hounds outgrew their threadbare wolf-suits.
Where the past-tense future took over.
Now he hides inside a clock tower
chiming every single solitary hour,
buying bread with watercolor dimes,
fearful of the way he walks
away from each waltz with seeds
splitting his rubber-soled shoes, step
after uneven step, falling one season
into whatever happens
to happen next.

You Don't Know Me Anymore

Talked to God again
this morning. He said work harder.
Leda leading her swan on a leash
while chemtrails slice the sky behind them.
He said heaven tames what it won't destroy
and I've kept too many memories:
glass moons, rusted license plates, dead flowers.
God said get rid of those. I didn't.
Sometimes he's handing out suggestions,
sometimes he's just being hyperbolic—
like the uncle who moves in
during hurricane season. Brings his knife
collection. Says to remain still
so the tornadoes don't see us,
to keep quiet so hurricanes can't hear.
He has a triangle tattooed over his heart.
Hecho en Sinaloa. Sometimes when I remember this,
I'm too young to understand. The preteen
living catty-corner on our street
was told by expensive doctors
to lose some weight. A tumor, darkening
in her stomach. Nine pounds. The size
of an overgrown newborn fawn.
Prom sparkles equally strangely. Blood
in the punchbowl, plastic stars
glued to the ceiling
that fell down in less than an hour, stuck
in girls' hair-sprayed bouffants. Two boys
left in handcuffs. God said get on with it.
This is where we come from, me and my uncle
who knocked up a girl when he was fourteen.
I never knew her name. One night, my uncle
sat beside me on the back porch, cricket choir
and silence rising from that Kansas ground
I took for granted. Torrid, stubborn rows of corn
refusing to turn their heads. And he released
one tear, wiped away

but not from my stained mind. A different girl before
and after. He showed me a picture
of someone he loved once, the heart-shaped face
which haunts me even now. My uncle
and I claim the same gray eyes,
bastard manners and baseless fears.
My uncle and I share hand-me-down scythes.
But God said not to be afraid. When
the world was predicted to end, we stayed
together while darkness turned
to daylight, turned to starlings, turned
to the silent expanse of sky which swallowed him, too.

REPRISE

Sometimes the house is underwater.
Sometimes it overlooks a marshland
blooming with mammoths. Sometimes
the house is empty, except for me.
I've lost something there, but
don't know what, or how to retrieve it.
My mother says my granddaughter
will dream of my house, too.
She'll make up stories about specters
inhabiting the halls, empty frames on walls,
the little wooden animals we hid
in silly places. I hope my mother
is wrong. I hope my granddaughter's dreams
are simple. I hope she visits me in a field
or the supermarket. Sometimes the house
is going up for sale in twenty minutes,
and I'm the only one around. Sometimes
I'm drowning by the time the dream starts.
Sometimes the pond has overwhelmed
the valley, making every blessed thing blue.
No. I hope my granddaughter doesn't dream
of me. I hope she dreams of delphiniums in bloom.

CHOKE

Black coffee. Brutal and bleak. Coins in a tin cup.
Brick bull, stick of butter, wicker basket.
Remember me as sunlit and grinning. No—
star-calling mystic. Pride sun. Envy moon.
Greed rising. Burn my body. Bury my urn
in the first known forest, piled with pine needles.
Crystalize the daylight. Gather maple leaves
when He's done breathing shivers through the trees.
Barefoot in the sand. Remember me as Woman With A Plan.
Remember me as Damsel Riding Bareback.
Define simultaneous. A door opened on its own.
Jealous sky casting out all its best angels.
Not mercy, but a plague.
Not salvation, but a warning.
Remember me as someone who couldn't stop attempting doorknobs.
Whisking my passion to whisps, body betraying
the bed of feathers, generous flowers I purposely misnamed:
Forget-You-Still. Lily of the Heartland. Black-Eyed Edith.
Trying to articulate the ordinary magic haunting every life—
even the devout cynic who still believes in soulmates.
Dearly departed, dear future tense, cruel past, blessed present—
remember me, who believed
our wooden-solid future's worth these temporary splinters.
Night owl screech. Footbridge holding steady.
Moonberry wine spilling over silver lips.
Clumsy love. Native tongue. Dark blue buttons on a blouse undone.
Hung there, draping across your perpetually empty chair.
Where women go to witness a million silent deaths.
Melody of refuge and silent nights. The peace in ceasefire.
Curled hair, hourless fear, sleeping with the lights on.
Shadows stuck to the sun like an unsinkable sickness.
The only illness light can't seem to shake. The unlikely
magnetism of extremes. Leaping from tree to tabletop
without anything attached at the wrist. Remember me
as translucent, tucking saviors in my waistband:

Peter Gabriel. Brigit Pegeen Kelly. Kevin Gates.
Yeah, I'd kick someone, too, if she got close to you.
Say you cared when I cried. Even now, you still do.
Learn the word lemniscate just to forget it. Remember me
as lost, one of the futile few. As always
recommitting to this disappearing act.
Remember me as an engine that never failed to start.
When you find yourself starving, resurrect me, just
so you can eat my strange volcanic heart.

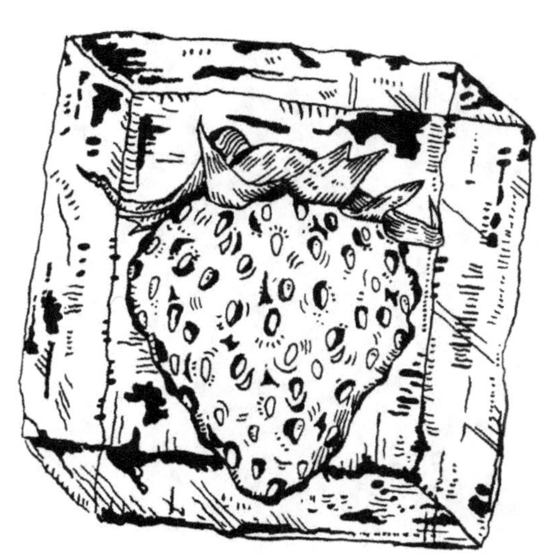

RIPPED MAPS, ROADKILL CARDINALS

And I tried to stop smoking but bought a new
            pack out of habit at every gas station
And I tried to confess my sins but buried bodies for more money instead
And I tried to get saved but couldn't read any roadsigns without sunlight
And I tried to open The Ozark Mountain Equestrian School for Dead Men
            but you won't believe what kind of clientele started showing up
And I tried to write down the true story but some
            men called my speaker self-absorbed, difficult, needy
And I tried to stop having needs but I was human
And I tried hard to love him but he didn't want me
And that's all I can say about why I don't enjoy autumn anymore

Today Merriam-Webster Dictionary Features the Words "Foible" and "Forte"

As in swords.

As in strength
        and weakness.

As in marriage.

As in anything
        silver-tipped.

As in Judas.

As in the second
        amendment.

As in *the opposite of a gun
        is wherever you point it.*

As in sitting on the stand
    as a young man with my father,
            canvas camouflage vests pulled
                tight around our chests, the cold
                    November air closing in around
                        us, when a sixteen-point buck
                            came into view, when I pulled
                                the trigger slow and steady like he
                                    showed me, and how the buck fell.

As in the field of memory.

As in burying our parents
        every generation.

As in peonies, fertility,
        infidelity.

As in knowing
        some men don't get to grow old.

As in the way Daunte Wright's name tastes like steel.

As in a white-picket fence
          reclaimed by ivy.

As in pinky promises
          we know won't be kept.

As in Congress.

As in the biggest cherry tree
          you've ever seen, perfect ruby
                    hearts smushed underfoot,
                              pits sticking in the grooves
                                        of a birdwatcher's boots.

As in the possibility of God.

As in peeling an orange,
          rind under your fingernails.

As in the Fourth of July sky
          exploding with fireworks.

As in long-stemmed roses.

As in saying a prayer
          over tonight's glass of whiskey.

As in the stick
          and gold of honey.

As in burning a flag
          when it becomes too tattered to fly.

As in waking up hungry.

As in seeing the end
          for what it is, or
                    could be: the beginning.

~III~

KALEIDOSCOPIC

THE MILLENIUM PROBLEM POEMS

Yang-Mills
Existence

So many stars between his ears. Mass gap
becoming non-trivial, quantifiable,
no longer arbitrary, undecidable,
sun-bleeding. Polynomials in a vacuum,
field theory, four-vector. He warned me
if the support of two
fields separate space-like, then
both are doomed to either commute
or anticommute—that spectrums, left unchecked, could twist themselves
into conical forms. An ever-shifting tornado.
Joplin, clouded in the distance. I can't stand an afterthought.
Diamonds breaking Neptune's silent surface.
Energy-momentum of natural disasters.
Pure light and positive numbers.
A void full of glue, glowing,
charged with his energy
in the absence of confinement.
Linear potential. The lightest particle.
That which requires proof yet goes an eternity without.

P VERSUS NP

PROBLEM

Lately she can't remove the armor, though.
Not even on her long walk back through
porches lamplit despite deadened
from summer's oppressive heat refusing
to settle groundward even at night. Nor the blisters
bleeding down the back of each heel
rubbing against loose shoes just barely too big, untied,
thigh burn and poison ivy rash, humid
cricket swarm and monsoon weather.
Even swollen moonlight. Even this
relentless emptiness.
Cataclysmic, kaleidoscopic. Polygamous stars. Collision course.
Three dimes for treason, one quarter
for a pay phone, if any could be found,
two cents for stolen opinions and singular nickel.
Hopscotch in hospital gowns.
For every game, a theory.
Every theory, ribbons unfurling—
deterministic headwaters, theoretical
polynomials, polygraphs, monotheistic
house of worship in the basement.
Natural disaster with the same name as her mother.
No escape for troublemakers.
Not even the Michelob bottle tops popped absent-
mindedly in the Missouri side's Mississippi cattails,
water rising, fear and sun spiraling, leather interiors,
floodplains dividing crucial parts of the smallest landscape on Earth.
Circle of wagons. Continue to tighten. Boa constrictor.
Not even the way she tries shaking off each flake of ash and
gloam. Belt or ouroboros—both consume endlessly.
For every sump pump overwhelmed, four basements
flooding. For every box of treasure lost at sea,
one empty flotsam chest floats finally home.

POINCARÉ

CONJECTURE

Even mathematicians know when
and how to interchange shapes
from one lacking alphabetic lexicon
for your brown-round language of the torus,
cello hollow, full of space, silent
in its continuum, curved nape of a clean-shaven neck, summertime
racetrack, horses nosing Kentucky Derby's finish line.
List of names written in lead. Dixon Ticonderoga again.
Two bucks on Daddy's Wildflower. Stranger
tells his brunette daughter they can only
sprint four furlongs. I spent so much time learning how to dance
while my father repeated the same thing
over and over. But some girls are born
with hearts where their ears should be.
Thin rubber band, expanding. Isosceles. Mandala.
Then my cat's cradle collapses. One door closes
while another swells to meet an inevitable riptide.
Just another hole in some unfirm ground.
        Only lost before found again.
Clockwise or forward. Heartache for breakfast.
Call me by my name. Girl in the Holocene.
I'm tearing down every stubborn, man-made brick
to bring you back to Earth, cursed moon. Eating nothing
but memories for dinner.
Bleary eyes, dessert. Feathers
sprouting weed-fast from his back, Icarus
leaps from his tower once
more, seafoam at the mouth, screaming
            Stay.

Navier-Stokes

But ultimately, all this remains theoretical. Figures
lingering in the margins of an overwhelmed page.
One page of thousands. Thousands among a mountain
white with unfinished manuscripts. Mistakes and molehills.
What we made versus what abandoned itself. Solutions
we let linger too long in the fire, just so we might
consume their ashes. Kindling thoughts. Midnight
and moonshine. Springtime wintering again. Even
when a fifth season arrived and we still didn't understand
how to conquer turbulence, harness the power of tears,
the smooth and steady snowfall, birch tree bark—
even when we beat back growing shadows, tooth
by gold-plated tooth, nail and voice volcanic, volumetric
force flowing down the free and incomprehensible path—
even then, we turned to find another horizon line sloping
into something neither of us—none
      of us—could bring ourselves to name.

BIRCH—SWINNERTON-DYER

CONJECTURE

Elliptic curve, one open problem in a field
of number theory, rolling down the emerald
hill of childhood, tumbling end over end
over finite end, animals in broad August,
antlers piercing cloudlight, Amazonian
fronds reaching down to break the otherwise perfect surface,
two forces out of motion becoming one
piece of art hung in the Louvre, rational,
L-functioned, prime numbered, paint and
poetry, the mathematics of an artist's life,
tenuous and complex, remarkable as a single blade of grass.

relative to blue lost in continental blue that blue yours or mine what blue could
be blue as blue could be blue torsion how i knew blue contortionist blue blue
how i knew before i knew blue blue the blue that followed dog in heat buzzing
blue panting blue collar crying blue fire blue string buzzing cello celtic buzzing
blue busy-eyed buzzard blue vultures swarming swimming in you blue blue i
swam in you blue you you you you never ended you that blue my blue
you never ended

Riemann

Hypothesis

Wild soft, wild sweet,
preening the fierce
green fever in me.
Felt the lightning brewing bold,
shattered teacup from the east.
Equations for answers.
Ring theory and dimes.
Hypnotized by cursive lines.
I follow you, you follow me,
the shake of shadows spiraling,
the confidence of continents,
inevitable sunrise holding steady.
A destiny of silent birds.
Riddle of snow, abrasion for chaos.
Overwhelmed by saltwater,
chrysanthemum courage,
the last wave of freefall.
Laced hands for necklaces.
Complex planes where functions
transform. Correspondences.
Wild, wild. Eye of the storm—
harmonic, enigmatic, theorizing,
future tense and vortex swirl,
elements reciprocating, gardens
of aether and earth-bound infinity.

HODGE

CONJECTURE

Horsepower in geometric spaces. Black hole.
Back nine at the country club. Cosmology for cynics.
One million dollars? For what? More candy? I can already
shake ripples across my skin one time then shapeshift into anything
you want. Answers? How many?
Study the topology of birds first, then every subvariety.
Peach trees blooming in some soft, possessed infinity.
Self defense against memories. Nighttime in Appalachia.
Hillbillies rejecting each bureaucratic elegy
written for them. Mountain mansions which overlook two rivers making love.
The place where barely-warm and frigid collide.
Break it apart. Break it open. How many dimensions
does a bad bitch need these days? One million
answers? For what? Something I can solve with my heart closed off?
You have to break the whole entire world. Build up the bomb.
Then let her drop.

PETALFALL

Q&A Question #61: Your Time Zone or Mine?

Take, for instance, the baby elephant's foot turned to a cigar case—
Escher's *Bond of Union*, Euler's *Seven Bridges*—
or forlorn Jesus hanging above the row of public urinals.
Meanwhile women have maintained our floral haven.
But you won't catch me discussing details. Not like that.
Think of how many dogs go through heaven's gate daily.
An old straw hat. The miniature civil war reenactment
      hiding behind display-case glass.
Collection, like love, kindles burden and sickness.
I wanted the world without knowing why,
to burn every fat cloud from our shared faultless sky.
Cheek bones, black keys, slender fingers tending.
Chicken livers, smoke pit, housewife Barbie.
I wanted to pull each shred of passion from corpses, even.
Back then I would've died to be buried alive.

Two Gods with Delusions of Grandeur

Petalfall and prairie sunrise, sing me sweet
or sweep low for angels weeping
all along the eastern seashore. You call heaven
cruel for sleeping while we wade wide water,
palms uncupped but holding all, pressed
together, diving again and deeper
each currentswell and tideshift,
every weatherturn and mudslide slippage,
fear abandoned near the treeline,
highways stretching above turgid rivers,
the shape of each body electrified in your headlights.
Shave away blonde braids for flesh.
Hang your sigil from my cursed, sleepless head
instead, your soul-creased halo, glowing
bright and merciful from within
by fate-instilled fire, turpentine, blue-bottled wine,
snowfall in the summertime, bad checks
bounced, dark-wisened valleys, brilliant hills
sparkling with silence, and the broken
concrete road that reached from here to there,
our long walk through nowhere.

DOG TRICKS

I shouldn't have gotten down on all fours during the church talent show
or invoked God
when really he was only a half-attentive parent
drinking a warm Coors Lite on the front porch
alongside other uninterested adult friends,
watching from the sides of His eyes
so no one got seriously injured.
I shouldn't have implied
His hand had anything to do with my hunger—but
what you have to understand is: at the time, I believed
He was with me. At the time,
I believed I could chase the tail straight off my body—
prayed every evening, even though
I never meant the whispered confessions, chased gray
to scare doctors away, avoided institutions
and getting institutionalized—
four-legged and fearful
of large nets and loud noises,
squealing-wheel-traumatized
gate-swinging escape artist
who believed
I could satisfy you
with only letters arranged the right way.
Then our skies divided. Then our waters darkened.
Then the gorges bloodied. Then puppy love turned to teeth.
When a pattern emerges, human nature demands
we start drawing lines between the stars
and deem our design something divine:
Orion. Ursa Minor. Canis Major.
The brightest star guiding men lost at night
belongs to an obedient guard dog. But
I'm wise enough now to forget
all the tricks you taught me
while I was lying
in the delicate hay of our making, rolling over

and over, shaking
the dust and decay of winter
from my body, constantly, expecting you
to come gladly through the field of faith and wildfire, whistling.

Strawberries

we shot three cows

then ran
desperate wolves

brothers through a field of berries

hidden in the bushes
a nest of bunnies

nearby an indifferent mower
and decapitated mother

swirl of green clippings
holographic lightning

the enormous hawk circling overhead
tulips turned away

we knew it was our fault
maybe not this
but something

sunlight's strand of pearls
on the edge of the forest

we stole the snow shovel
stowed our shadows in the garage
set fire to the barn

we did those things

two kids riding shoulder-to-shoulder
shotgun in a doorless datsun

then life's glass tunnel tightened
and our mother disappeared too

the way all parents do

the day she died
each cloud was milk-white

when we woke
alongside one another

we were only boys

two loose needles
without a haystack to hide inside

sensing the storm
before it arrived

WILDERNESS

You call to me and I go.
I leave my compass; I know North.
I leave my rosary; my faith is in
your Aurora Borealis. I'll follow
your light through the foothills.
The spines of leaves shiver, emerald
pools show me
the way. I pray. For you,
I'd catch a fish in my teeth.
I hear you howl from the mountain;
I crawl on hands and knees, sniffing
the air, feeling the quiver of the earth.

Q&A Question #64: How Do You Feel Now?

Vascular anomaly. Atomic fissure. Rift theory—
cabinet of curiosities, atrocities, hydrogen bombs.
Where pressure meets fission. Seven fisherwomen
intricately whittled into a fossilized hornbill's skull.
Combat with gardening tools. Hand to bloody hand.
Two-headed calf, three-hearted lamb. Bell jar full of honeybees.
Mannequin missing both legs laid to rest
       against the concrete median dividing
the highway that reaches from his town back into mine.
Hard to find a reason for staying anywhere anymore—
pile of horse hair, stack of loose ends.
No graveyards for plastic people. No funerals for fake friends.
No sugar in the tea they serve before severing all my limbs.
Stereo versus static. Tasmanian tree fern. Newt poles circle
an antique teapot. *They like it in there.* Such reassurance.
A massive clam shell split open to cradle children's shoes.
All I ever wanted was to deliver you from
       the sure, swift loneliness of growing old as an only child.
Ceramic model of two men butchering the mother pig.
Stuffed goat with a belt around its throat. Elevator music.
Threadbare top hats decorating our church's decommissioned piano.
Whaling ship which outgrew her bland bottle, splintered
glass and delicate, webbed fractures. Even
this starlight, outlasting us all, threatening
to fall from the very sky we pray to—good
God, good fucking Lord—if you can spare no more
mercy, please, at least
save what I never could.

CUANDO

And when it comes down on me, Moses, let it be
in the form of centuried moss. Let it be the shape of fire.
Let it be slow as the doe crossing my grandfather's river.
Let it be the river. Let it be the doe.

POWER OF WOMEN

Notes and Acknowledgments

Thank you, first and every time, to Katie Erbs—sister, comrade, and Editor of Deez.

Dorianne, Shara, Danusha, Kwame, Joe, Mike, Kellie, Valerie, Rita, Sarah, Karen, Karla, Bruce, Murray, Meg, Paul, Don, Ralph, Shane. Every day for the rest of my life, and then some.

Atina, Rana, Allison, Mac, Verena, Palmer, Keeley, Rebekah, Emily, Paul, Joyce, Hahn, Itaya, Rana, Kasper, Tony, Kyle, Cindy, Brennan, Abbey, Claire, Olivia, Keara, Mel, Symone, Chad, Nigel, Will, Nick . . . and company. My crew! Thank you always.

Anne, Melissa, Bryan, Tim and Barb, Bob, Scott and Jennifer, various scholarships and funds, the Riggins and Mohesky families, the Esop and Wylie families. David Clewell. None of this would exist without you.

Mom and Dad: I finally found that marketable skill. Thanks for being patient!

HESK.

Previous versions of the works selected for *Flowermouth* have appeared in publications by, though potentially not limited to, the following: *October Hill Magazine*; *Bullshit Lit*; *The Racket Journal*; *Litmora*; *Rinnan Lit.*; *Pink Apple Press*; *Dollar Store Magazine*; *Nebulous Magazine*; *Requiem for Daisyworld*, housed in the Tim and Cathy Tran Library in Forest Grove, Oregon; Webster University's *Green Fuse* Literary Magazine; *The Ozark Mountain Equestrian Club for Dead Men* (limited run*)*; *Too Close to the Fire* (limited run); and more.

"Today Merriam Webster Dictionary Features the Words 'Foible' and 'Forte'" features the phrase "the opposite of a gun is wherever you point it" which has been borrowed from Brendan Constantine's poem *The Opposite Game*. Thanks, Brendan, for imagining this phrase so accurately.

If you, dear reader, are one of the lucky few who managed to obtain *The Ozark Mountain Equestrian Club for Dead Men* before its untimely demise, you will certainly recognize some of the poems in this collection. As the aforementioned work is no longer available for purchase in its original format through no fault of the author, who has retained all rights to reproduction, we agreed as a team that the appropriate decision was to provide this work to the general public in a permanently accessible format. Therefore: please enjoy this edition, lovingly referred to as Kate's Version.

Thank you to every reader, whether you're just picking up these poems for the first time, or if you're enjoying them for the thirtieth. They breathe for you.

I love you, the one whose eyes fall here, across this very sentence. Thank you for reading.

And thank God for yet another necessary course correction.

for my parents

and patricia

www.ingramcontent.com/pod-product-compliance
Lightning Source LLC
Chambersburg PA
CBHW072122150726

47999CB00005B/2082